THE
MINOTAUR

MONSTERS OF MYTHOLOGY

25 VOLUMES

Hellenic

Amycus
Anteus
The Calydonian Boar
Cerberus
Chimaera
The Cyclopes
The Dragon of Beotia
The Furies
Geryon
Harpalyce
Hecate
The Hydra
Ladon
Medusa
The Minotaur
The Nemean Lion
Procrustes
Scylla and Charybdis
The Sirens
The Spear-birds
The Sphinx

Norse

Fafnir
Fenris

Celtic

Drabne of Dole
Pig's Ploughman

MONSTERS OF MYTHOLOGY

THE
MINOTAUR

Bernard Evslin

CHELSEA HOUSE PUBLISHERS

New York   Philadelphia   New Haven

EDITOR
Jennifer Caldwell

ART DIRECTOR
Giannella Garrett

PICTURE RESEARCHER
Susan Quist

DESIGNERS
Carol McDougall, Noreen Lamb

CREATIVE DIRECTOR
Harold Steinberg

First Printing

Library of Congress Cataloging-in-Publication Data

Evslin, Bernard.
The Minotaur.

(Monsters of mythology ; bk. 2)
Summary: Recounts the Greek myth about the monster
with the head of a bull and the body of a man, which
lived in the Labyrinth in Crete until killed by the
hero Theseus.
1. Minotaur (Greek mythology)—Juvenile literature.
[1. Minotaur (Greek mythology) 2. Theseus (Greek
mythology) 3. Mythology, Greek] I. Title. II. Series:
Evslin, Bernard. Monsters of mythology ; bk. 2.
BL820.M63E97   1987   398.2'1   86-24524

ISBN 1-55546-237-5

Printed i n Singapore

For my son, Tom
who tracks numbers down labyrinthine ways,
and now has a young Daedalus on his hands,
even as his father did. . .

So, of course, this is also for his son,
Jarah Evslin

Characters

Monster

The Minotaur (MIHN oh tor)	Half man, half bull, wholly fatal

Cretans

Minos (MEE nohss)	King of Crete; Emperor of the Lands of the Middle Sea
Ariadne (air ih AD nee)	His daughter, a maiden acquainted with magic
Phaedra (FEE druh)	His younger daughter; her sister's rival
Europa (yoo ROH puh)	His mother, a Phoenician princess abducted by Zeus
Pasiphae (PAS ih fy)	His wife; mother of Ariadne, Phaedra, and the Minotaur

Athenians

Theseus (THEE see uhs)	Prince of Athens; a hard-riding, easy-spoken young hero
Aegeus (EE jee uhs)	King of Athens; supposed father of Theseus
Aethra (ETH ruh)	Queen of Athens; seduced by Poseidon; mother of Theseus
Daedalus (DEHD uh luhs)	Born in Athens but dwelling in Crete; most brilliant inventor of ancient times, or any time
Icarus (IHK uh ruhs)	His son, also talented

Gods

Zeus (ZOOS)	King of the Gods, Lord of the Sky, wielder of thunder and lightning; appearing here first as a bull and then in his own radiant form
Poseidon (poh SY duhn)	God of the Sea, who sired Theseus during one high tide
Aphrodite (af ruh DY tee)	Goddess of Love and Beauty, particularly to be feared when answering prayers

Others

The Barley-hag	A prophetic crone
Thera (THEE ruh)	A sea nymph who sings to Theseus of battles to come

Contents

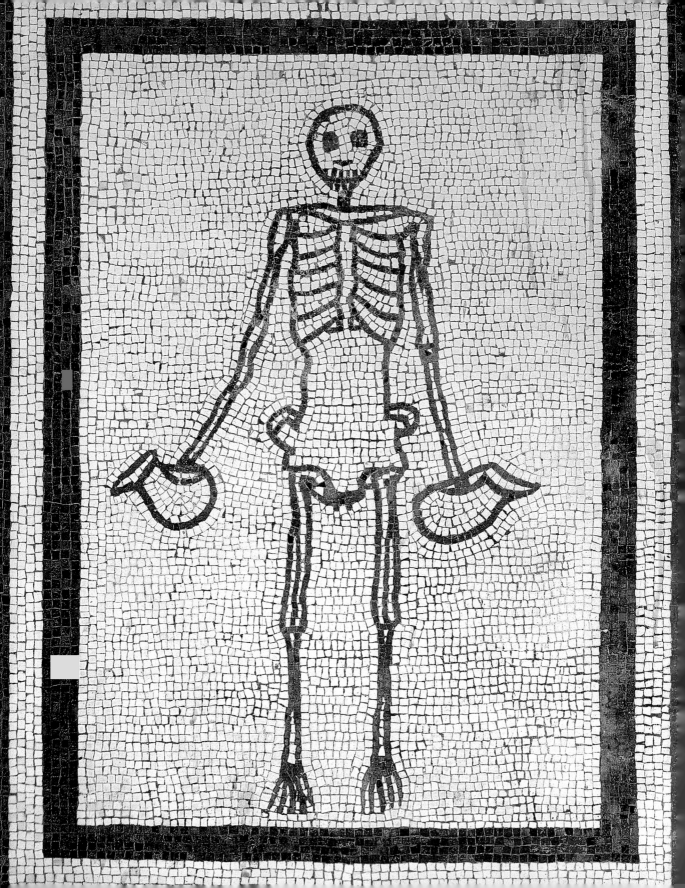

1

The Singing Bones

he meadow around the maze was a huge velvety sward tended by gardeners who knew they would be thrown to the Minotaur if they allowed one blade of grass to grow too long.

Two girls were chasing each other over the green, but swerved suddenly and ran toward the outer hedge of the Labyrinth—a deadly puzzle-garden on the island of Crete. The bellowing had stopped, which meant that the killing had started. There was a pulsing hush, then the screaming began. It rose to a shriek, a horrid, anguished din scarcely muffled by the hedges—then fell to moaning and the gurgling coughs from gut wounds.

"It's mean not to let us watch," said Phaedra.

"Nothing to see," said the taller girl, whose name was Ariadne. "They aren't Athenians or anything. Just people Papa's tired of."

"I'd still like to."

"It never lasts long, you know. Those prisoner types are too scared to fight back."

"It's all right for you to talk," said Phaedra. "You've seen it all, selfish cat."

"Shut up or I'll slap you. I might anyway."

Phaedra started to run away. "Wait," said Ariadne.

"Why? So you can slap me?" said the younger sister.

"I won't if you're not pesky. Wait till the Hag comes. We'll get our fortunes told."

"Stupid old hag," said Phaedra. "She gets everything all wrong."

"There's a new one, the Barley-hag. A real witch."

"Do you believe that?"

"Well, she's something weird. They beat her with staves in the usual way and broke every bone in her body. And when they were through, she got up and walked away. It's never happened before. Now people are mad for her to tell their fortunes because she goes around singing, 'If you won't die, you don't lie. . . .' But she hasn't told anybody's yet."

"How do you know she'll do yours?" asked Phaedra.

"She wants something. She was hanging around the castle this morning when I came out. 'Wait for me in the meadow,' she said. 'I'll come to you when the killing's done.' So I'm waiting, but you don't have to."

"Maybe she'll do me too."

"Don't ask her until she's through with me," said Ariadne.

"All right, all right . . ."

A squad of the King's Guard trotted past. Picked for their size, the biggest youths in the kingdom, they wore brass breastplates, brass shingreaves, and heavy brass helmets. They were basting in their own sweat under the hot sun. The guards despised such summer duty, but no one dared grumble. Minos had ordered full armor, and they preferred being broiled in brass to being served raw to the Minotaur.

The girls spotted the Hag sidling through the hedge that formed the outer wall of the Labyrinth. She limped toward them, a small, hunched figure in the vast meadow. She carried a sack over her shoulder. The girls waited, watching her slow, crippled walk. When she reached them, she dropped the sack on the

ground with a crash. She blinked up at them. She was incredibly ugly, almost bald, and the clumps of hair that clung to her head looked like mildew. Her nose and chin almost met over the toothless hole that was her mouth. But her eyes were bright bubbles, like a squirrel's eyes. She curtsied and her rag skirt billowed in the breeze.

"Ah, my pretties, my dearies, are you waiting for the Hag, then?" She began to cackle, but it turned into coughing.

"You told me to wait," said Ariadne. "So here I am."

"And here *she* is," cried the crone, pointing to Phaedra. "Here we are, all three—the royal girls and me! Hee, hee, hee! Someone carry my sack, please, and we'll go up the hill. If I carry it, I'll cough myself away."

"Phew, it stinks!" said Phaedra. "What's in it?"

"Bones, old bones . . . gathered from the killing ground. I need my tattlebones, don't I?"

Ariadne snatched the sack from her sister and raced away over the meadow. "See you on the hilltop," she called. Phaedra stayed with the old woman and they followed the girl as she bounded up the slope.

From the crown of the hill they looked down on a burning stretch of sea. "Hang the bones," said the Hag. "Do it properly— skull on top, ribs just so, armbones hanging, legs below . . . and the skeleton will dance to a skeletune by the yellow light of a hangman's moon . . ."

The girls emptied the sack and hung the bones from the branch of a wild olive tree. The skeleton hung in the red light of the falling sun. Phaedra started to say something, but the Hag put her fingers to her lips, and the girl fell silent. Ariadne had not uttered a word since climbing the hill. The Hag raised her arm and called out:

> West wind, west wind,
> howl and moan.
> West wind, west wind,
> sing through bone.
>
> West wind, west wind,
> when you blow,
> tell us what
> we need to know.

Light ruffled the water as a wind arose. The bones swayed, rattled, and did a dry jig. Ariadne closed her eyes. She couldn't bear to look at the dancing bones. She felt herself seized by a nameless fury and wanted to kill them both, sister and hag. She began to stalk over the grass toward them, then froze. For the wind was blowing through the skull, making it sing:

> Tigers are wild,
> dogs are tame.
> Listen, dear child,
> to your husband's name.
>
> Theseus, Theseus.
> A prince for a princess,
> Theseus is his name.
>
> Roses are red,
> wounds are too.
> Him you shall wed,
> I tell you true.

Ariadne stared out to sea. She felt her face stiffen as if it were carved of bone, as hard and salty as the skull dangling from the tree. Phaedra sat mesmerized on the grass. She reached up and tugged at the Hag's skirt.

"Do me," she whispered.

The Hag bent to her, put her withered lips to the girl's shell-pink ear, and whispered, "Shall I tell you your husband's name?"

"Yes, yes!"

"Hush. . . . She mustn't hear . . . or she'll kill you," said the Hag.

"Why?"

"Because the name you shall hear is the name you have heard."

"What do you mean?" said Phaedra.

"The lad you shall marry is named Theseus."

"Two with the same name?"

"*One* with the same name . . . who shall marry a pair of sisters, the eldest first. Farewell now."

The Hag vanished.

2

Son of the Sea God

Young Theseus had two fathers—an official one named Aegeus who was King of Athens—and a real father, whom he had never met and whom his mother had met only once. He was Poseidon, Lord of the Sea, a huge, brawling, piratical god, whose favorite sport was riding a tidal wave in to some seaside village where a wedding was being held. Green-bearded and roaring with laughter, he would rise from the swirling waters to snatch the bride from the arms of her half-drowned groom. But he would always return her the next morning; he liked wet brides, but didn't want them to dry into wives. As for his children, he was very content to let someone else care for them.

Poseidon had raided the wedding party of the Fisher King, Aegeus, and borrowed his bride. She gave birth to a child named Theseus. For the son of a god, he was unusually small, but he was very quick and graceful, and he swam like an otter before he could walk. His eyes, too, told of the sea. They were not quite green, not quite blue, and only sometimes gray, changing with his mood as the water changes when the wind blows.

Theseus had no way of knowing that he had been sired by a god, but he did know that he was different from other boys. Others fought because they wanted something someone else had, or wanted to keep what someone else wanted. But Theseus fought because he enjoyed it and always challenged those larger than himself, who were not very hard to find. He fought without rancor but with a wild élan and disregard for pain. And, despite his size, he usually won.

As a son of Poseidon, he had another inborn talent—horse-manship. All of the sea god's horde of children were magnificent riders. For, as it happened, in the first days of his reign, Poseidon had been especially fond of Demeter, the tall, abundant goddess, Queen of Harvests, whose fall of hair was like wheat ripening in the sun, whose voice was the throstling of birds at dawn, and in whose footsteps flowers sprang. The sea god doted on her and pursued her whenever he was not occupied with something else.

One day, as Demeter was scattering seeds on a small, fertile island some miles off the mainland, Poseidon leaped out of the sea and raced toward her. She fled across a meadow. But he caught her, twined a rope of enormous freshwater pearls about her neck, and demanded that she love him.

Demeter didn't know what to do; he was so huge, so lavish, so laughingly insistent.

"Prove your love," she said. "Give me another gift."

"Another?"

"Not something oysters made, but something you have labored over yourself, thinking of me all the while."

"What do you want?"

"You have made many creatures for the sea. Now make me a land animal. But a beautiful one. More beautiful than any other animal on land, or sea, or air."

Demeter thought she was safe, believing Poseidon could make only monsters. Much to her amazement and delight, he presented her with a horse. Poseidon so admired his own hand-iwork that he immediately made a herd of horses that galloped about the meadow, tossing their manes, prancing and neighing their pleasure. Poseidon was so fascinated by the horses that he forgot all about Demeter for the moment, leaped on one, and rode off. Later, he made another herd of green surf horses for his

Green-bearded and roaring with laughter, Poseidon would rise from the swirling waters to snatch the bride from the arms of her half-drowned groom.

own stables. But Demeter kept her own gift, and from that herd all the horses in the world have descended.

One story says that it took Poseidon an entire month to make one horse. His first attempts weren't to his liking and he simply cast them away. These creatures made their way into the world. They were the camel, the hippopotamus, the giraffe, the donkey, and the zebra.

Afterward, through some twist of inheritance, all the sea god's children could ride before they could walk; all became ardent horsemen and horsewomen, especially Theseus.

But now, in this year of change that was crowning his boyhood, Theseus had begun to ride other creatures, more difficult than horses. He climbed on bulls and learned to ride them, though he suffered many a painful fall. Finally, he could sit on any bull, even the wild ones. He sneaked up on deer as they grazed, leaped on the backs of stags, and rode them—they ran swiftly and leaped to dizzy heights. But deer were far easier to ride than bulls.

Theseus tried something even more difficult. In the early morning, he would race across the meadow, dive into the sea, and slide aboard slippery dolphins. They could always get rid of him by going underwater. But they were playful, gallant creatures and soon accepted this as a game. Leaping straight up out of the water, the dolphins tried to shake him off. Soon, he was able to cling to them, no matter what they did, and became confident that he could ride any creature in the world.

One morning after a gale, Theseus was prowling the beach, for storm brings many treasures for a boy to find. He spotted something flashing on top of a rock. He came closer and saw that it was a silver comb held by a hand at the end of a bronzed arm. A sea nymph sat on the rock, combing her long, green hair.

He approached slowly, then climbed the rock. The nymph arose and towered above him on long, bronzed legs. He laughed with pleasure. "Good morning," he said.

She sat again, dangling her legs over the edge. "Good morning, Theseus."

"You know my name. . . ."

"I do."

"May I know yours?"

"Thera."

"Are you a Nereid?"

"I am."

"Are they all as beautiful as you?"

She smiled at him. "You're sweet."

"May I kiss you?"

He put his arm on her warm shoulder. He felt that it was stuck there, that he could never pull it away. She shrugged him off.

"You're pretty sassy for a sprout. I might smack you."

"Well, do something to me, for goodness sake. We're wasting our youth. Nymph, sweet nymph, why don't you teach me to swim?" said Theseus.

"You don't know how? Wasn't it you I saw riding a dolphin the other day? Don't lie."

"Well . . . maybe I can swim a little. But you could improve my stroke."

"You're a true son of your father, aren't you?"

"My father?"

"Poseidon. No Nereid is safe when he's around."

"I don't know what you're raving about," said Theseus. "My father is King Aegeus, a nice, safe old man."

"All right, if you say so. Would you like me to sing to you?"

"May I sit on your lap?"

"Sit where you are! Well, you can lie back and put your head on my lap."

Theseus leaned back and nestled his head on her lap—the most delicious cushion a head could have. Tears of joy filled his eyes as a wild caramel musk of sun and sea rose about him. She began to sing, and her voice was like the wind at dusk crooning over the waves as it comes bearing cool airs to the parched land:

Sisters two
for you to woo
if you do
what you're fated to.
Beware, beware
the bull-man's horn,
or your blood will feed
the Cretan corn.

Like a spider,
but immensely wider,
the Minoan Bull
has blood to shed.
And you must ply
the antic thread,
lest the monster
leave you dead.

You shall meet
on evil Crete,
where sisters two
wait for you.

Shall you dare
that fatal pair,
of butcher-king
and mad queen born?
Beware, beware
the monster's horn,
or your blood will feed
the Cretan corn.

"Are you a Nereid?"
  "I am."
    "Are they all as beautiful as you?"

Woman in Profile (1898–99) by Gustav Klimt

Theseus felt her voice pulling him down into fathoms of sleep. The song was the skeleton of his dream, and the dream was full of terror. Demon girls were after him, and a bull-man was goring him. Everywhere there was blood. There was pain. There was fear. But his head was in the nymph's lap and her musk was about him, her voice weaving the dream. He knew then that she had been sent to tell him of something dreadful that was to happen to him later. Her song was a warning. But she had brought him a new kind of joy, one that made him see everything differently. The boy, who was to become a hero, suddenly knew then what most heroes learn later—and some too late—that joy blots suffering and that the road to nymphs is beset by monsters.

The tide had come in and was swirling about the foot of the rock. The nymph arose, clasping his wrists in one hand and his ankles in the other, then lifted him above her head with amazing strength. She tilted his face to hers, kissed him on the lips, and tossed him into the sea.

Falling, he straightened into a dive and split the water cleanly. When he surfaced, the rock was bare. Far out he saw bronzed shoulders gleaming on the sea. He swam a few strokes after her, then turned back to shore. She was, like a dolphin, not to be caught until she wanted to be.

3

The Tyrant

o understand what is happening, and why, we must go back two generations, to the birth of Minos. He had a first-class pedigree. His father was Zeus, King of the Gods, who abducted a young Phoenician princess named Europa. Zeus often fancied mortal maidens, but had learned to be careful. If he appeared to them first in his true form, so bright and terrible, they were liable to get burned to ashes. This finally taught Zeus how inflammable girls could be. Now, he was determined that nothing should happen to the beautiful Europa before he could embrace her. So he appeared to her not in his own form, but as a huge white bull.

He came onto the Phoenician beach where Europa was playing ball with her handmaidens. She caroled with joy when she saw the splendid animal, and was amazed to see him kneel on the sand as if inviting her to climb on his back. "Be careful!" cried the maidens, but Europa was a high-spirited, reckless girl. Without hesitation, she leaped onto the bull. The giant beast arose

The maidens screamed in horror to see the huge white bull swim toward the setting sun with Europa clinging to his back.

and galloped away into the sea. The maidens screamed in horror to see him swim toward the setting sun with Europa clinging to his back.

After a while the girl stopped sobbing and began to enjoy her adventure. No girl in the world, she thought, would be able to match the tale she would have to tell when she returned to her father's court.

But Europa never returned. Zeus changed back to his own form and took her to a cave gouged into the side of Crete's Mount Ida. His daughters, the Hours, had hung rich tapestries and carpeted the cave with flowers, making it a fragrant bridal chamber.

Zeus stayed with Europa for a week, planted a son in her, and left, promising to return.

Now, Zeus was Zeus, and Europa was a fine, big, healthy girl, but their first son, for some reason, began life as a miserable bluish scrap of flesh, too feeble even to cry. Europa fought hard to keep him alive. She was happy that Zeus did not visit her. She did not want him to see their son, whom she had named Minos. Europa did not know whether the baby would live—she did not even know whether she wanted him to, but she kept fighting for his life.

Minos pulled at his mother's breast, drank the strong milk, and survived. He lived, but he did not flourish. When he was a year old, Europa could still hold him in the palm of her hand, and did not dare to wean him. She was still nursing him when he was two years old. He could walk and talk but was still tiny, and would take nothing but her milk. Zeus came to the cave in Crete upon occasion. He never inquired about the child and she never mentioned him. She hid Minos away when she knew Zeus was coming.

Europa found herself pregnant again, and knew she would have to stop nursing her firstborn. She tried to wean him. But he climbed her leg and stood on her knee, saying in his silvery little voice:

"Mother, I require suckle."

He tugged at her tunic, encircling her breast with both arms, and began nursing happily.

Europa bore her second child, again a boy, but how different he was. This was a superb, big one, looking every bit the son of a god. His eyes streamed light, and there seemed to be laughter in his first cry. Europa immediately fell in love with him, which made it easy for her to reach a decision about Minos. She denied him her milk. When Minos began to howl, she carried him to the cow byre, where dwelt a big young heifer, her udders bursting with milk. Europa sat him on the straw under the cow and went back to the cave to nurse her beautiful new son.

Minos howled with fury, but nobody came. For the first time, his mother did not rush to comfort him. He was bewildered, and his untried heart grew ripe with hatred. But most of all he was hungry.

"Mother, Mother!" he shrieked.

No one came. The cow swerved her head and nuzzled the little boy. Her big tongue was warm upon his naked body. He shivered at the new sensation. It was warm and fragrant in the byre. There was a reek of hay and fresh milk. He pressed against the cow's muzzle, wanting her to lick him again. She yawned. Her breath was heavy and beautiful, as if she had been eating flowers. He was small enough to walk beneath her. He went to her udder and patted the warm bag of milk. The cow mooed; the whole byre hummed with her sound. She was ready to be milked.

Minos drank from her udder. It was not like his mother's milk; it was sweet and creamy and strange. He almost gagged, but he was hungry. He swallowed the first mouthful and pulled at the teat. The cow lowed. Her tail swished. . . . And there in the warm darkness, in the smell of hay and the rich strangeness of change, Minos sank into sleep.

Now Crete was a privileged island. Remote, reef-girded, and lovely, it was a favorite trysting place for Zeus. Its animals had not been deprived of speech. So it was that a wolf that had been prowling about the cow byre pounced upon Minos as he came out wiping his milky lips, and snarled: "Well met! You shall be my breakfast."

"You treat yourself shabbily, my friend," said Minos, thinking quickly. "See how small I am—just a little scrap of nothing, as my mother calls me."

"Better than nothing," growled the wolf.

"Scarcely," said Minos. "But I can guide you to a fine meal. Inside that cave is a remarkably tasty child—plump, tender, and delicious—brother of mine, as a matter of fact."

"You're trying to trick me," said the wolf. "Surely such a child does not lie untended."

"My mother is also in there," said Minos, "but soon she will go to the stream to fetch water."

"How do I know you're telling the truth?"

"No need to trust me. You can keep me here under your paw until you see my mother come out of the cave."

The wolf slunk back into the shadow of a rock, dragging Minos with him. He kept the child pinned to the ground as he watched the mouth of the cave. A tall girl came out, lightly bearing a heavy yoke across her shoulders. Minos, peering out from under the wolf's paw, saw that his mother looked happier than he had ever seen her.

"Wait until she goes down that path, out of sight," he whispered to the wolf. "Then, into the cave!"

When Europa came back to her rock chamber, she found the wooden cradle empty. It was still swaying slightly on its rockers. She rushed out, screaming, and looked everywhere. All day she searched, under every rock, every bush. She couldn't find any tracks; the ground was too stony. It grew dark. Then she remembered her other child and rushed to the byre.

On the way she heard a little snuffling sound, and saw Minos lying on the ground, sobbing.

"Oh, Mother, Mother," he cried when she knelt to him. "I saw a terrible thing. A wolf running by, holding my dear brother in his jaws. 'Stop!' I yelled. 'Take me instead; my mother loves him better.' But the wolf growled, 'It's him I want; he's fatter,' and ran off. Mother, Mother, where were you? Where were you?"

Europa gathered him into her arms and they wept together. That night when he crawled into her lap, mewing piteously, she

That night when Minos crawled into her lap, Europa gave him her breast . . . and kept him there all night, nestled against her.

gave him her breast, which was aching with undrunk milk. She kept him there all night, nestled against her.

The next morning, Europa climbed to the top of the highest mountain in Crete and uttered the eagle scream that Zeus had bade her use as a signal in times of dire trouble. A huge white eagle swooped down to the crag where she stood and took the form of Zeus. She threw herself into his arms, crying: "Oh, my master, plant another child in me, I pray. For the beautiful son you have given me is dead."

"You seem a bit careless with your children, my dear. I have never seen the first one at all. And now, it seems, I am not to know the second one. Are you sure you want to try again?"

"Please, my lord . . ."

Zeus still wore the enormous white wings of the eagle. It was midsummer, high noon. Zeus and Europa seemed to be inside a great golden bell humming with light. He spread his white wings, shielding her from the sun's glare and from his wife's vigil. He leaned forward and pressed her to the earth.

The shadows grew long and blue. A breeze stroked them. Zeus spoke: "You have kept the first boy from my sight. I know your intention was good, but the time has come for father and son to meet. Fetch him."

"Yes, my lord."

Europa went down the mountain and came up again, bearing Minos on her shoulder. She faced Zeus in the curdling red light of the sunset and held the naked boy out to him.

"Behold, your son."

Zeus studied the child. He saw a tiny face cocked toward him, alert as a bird's, wary but unafraid.

"Runty, to be sure," muttered Zeus, "but vicious, greedy, and clever—qualities often enlarged by smallness."

"Bless me, Father," said the boy.

"The blessing rests with you, my son. You shall be a king and master of kings, if first you master yourself."

Zeus studied the child. . . . "The blessing rests with you, my son.
You shall be a king and master of kings."

"Thank you, sire."

"I do not wish to hear of another accident happening to any brother or sister of yours."

"Now that we have become acquainted, mighty father, I feel that our family fortunes must improve."

*Minos made himself king of Crete . . . and he made
cattle the pivotal symbols of his state religion.*

"Take care, Minos. I am not to be jested with, or disobeyed."

"Full gravely shall I follow your commandments, Father."

"Your mother will bear again—more than once. I commend those children to your care."

"They will find me a tender and watchful brother, my lord."

"Farewell."

Zeus spread his wings and flew away.

Minos did obey his father, and in time was rewarded by becoming a man whom others obeyed. One by one he exterminated every aspirant to the Cretan throne, and made himself king. He then began to attack the other lands of the Middle Sea. He married the princess Pasiphae, and she bore him two daughters, Ariadne and Phaedra.

Minos knew that he was hated, and he was content in that knowledge. A beloved king was a weak king to be loudly mourned, as he was insufficiently obeyed. Minos did not wish to be loved; he wanted to be feared. And he was. But if he was heartless toward humans, he was kind to beast and bird, especially cherishing cattle, for which he bore an abiding love. Indeed, he made them the pivotal symbols of his state religion.

Minos invoked his parents, the White Bull and the Phoenician princess, decreeing a reenactment of Europa's abduction as the central rite of the Minoan creed. He ordered that a special corps of vestals be trained to serve the Horned Moon—the Cow Goddess, whose milk was rain—and appointed his daughter, Ariadne, to the sisterhood of priestesses. Whatever he did flourished. He not only wielded temporal power but dominated the priesthood of a successful religion, rich in murder and orgy, appealing to the mob and useful to the throne.

He encouraged public executions. The dungeon cells were thronged with those who had offended Minos or one of his current favorites, and the leather-aproned headsmen wielded their double axes overtime to make space for new prisoners.

4

Aphrodite's Vengeance

n the seventh year of his reign, when he had established absolute rule in Crete, Minos made a move that was to turn him from king to emperor. He invited the great Athenian inventor Daedalus to come to Crete, offering him great wealth for his labors.

Daedalus accepted and was royally welcomed when he came to the island. Minos presented him with the most lavishly equipped workshop in the entire world and gave him strong slaves and clever apprentices. The king also made his wishes clear.

"You have been creating tools of peace," he told Daedalus. "You have given mankind the ox-yoke, the plough, and the loom, all of which are very useful. But I want you to concentrate on the tools of war. Weapons, man, I need weapons that will make me invincible on land and sea."

By this time Daedalus had formed a good idea of the person he had sold his talent to, and did not dare disobey. Besides, he was extremely comfortable in the brilliant capital of Knossos, and he had never much cared how his inventions were used, as long as they worked.

So he did as Minos asked, and weapon after fearsome weapon issued from his workshop. He began by providing a unique sentry to patrol the wild sections of the coast. He devised a living statue and cast it in bronze. Talos, he called it, and there was never a sentinel like this one: a giant humanoid figure, tall as a tree, invulnerable to sword, spear, or arrow, and completely obedient to whomever Daedalus designated. Talos circled the island three times a day. Whenever a galley approached, Talos hurled huge boulders at it, sinking it or driving it off.

Then followed a stream of weapons. Giant catapults. Chariots whose hubs were whirling scythes that could winnow a rank of armored men like a reaper moving through a stand of wheat.

Minos was very pleased. He couldn't stop praising his inventor, who became recognized as the most important person at court next to the king.

But not all of Daedalus's creations were so grim. In the intervals of his labor, he found time to make a sisterhood of dancing dolls for the king's daughters, who visited his workroom with their mother, Pasiphae. He made other marvelous toys—a perfume flask that played music when uncorked, and a parasol, lighter than a butterfly's wing, that opened like a flower when it felt the sun. He enjoyed these visits mightily. Pasiphae was beautiful, and her two little girls were exquisite. All three were very affectionate to the one who made them such wonderful gifts.

But one day Daedalus and Pasiphae held a conversation that was to have dreadful consequences.

"Tell me, Athenian," said Pasiphae, stretching her long, bare arms and yawning. "Do you think I'm good-looking?"

"My queen, I'm supposed to have a reasonable command of the language, but am quite unable to describe how beautiful I think you are."

"Try."

"You are simply the most gorgeous woman I have ever met or could hope to meet."

"How about Aphrodite? Am I as beautiful as she is?"

"I've never had the privilege of meeting the goddess."

"Well, you've seen statues of her. If the sculptors are getting it right, she's a big cow—the kind my husband's always chasing. Well, he has an excuse, I suppose; his foster mother was a cow, as he's told me a million tedious times. Don't you think she's a bit bovine, that Aphrodite? I'm of pretty good size myself, but those hips of hers. *Massive*, my dear!"

"Try to be discreet, sweet lady, I beg you. The gods are quick to take offense."

"Do you really think there are such things as gods—an intelligent, sophisticated man like you? I think they're all nursery tales and nonsense."

"Your husband. . ."

Daedalus's improvements made the ships of Crete swifter and more maneuverable by far than any that had ever sailed the waters of the world.

"Oh, I know, I know; his father was Zeus, who changed into a white bull and came up on the beach after Europa, who didn't have the sense not to ride strange bulls. . . ."

"You don't believe that?" asked Daedalus.

"Oh my, don't you know anything about politics? Don't you know that any little village chieftain who wants to enlarge his domain begins by blowing up his pedigree?"

"My queen, you are witty as you are beautiful, and as reckless. I don't consider myself superstitious, but I have had

. . . viewing herself in this wondrous glass. . .
Aphrodite would be able to see the back of her head.

personal experience with the vengeful gods, and I beg you not to mock them."

"I'm bored, Daedalus—bored, bored, bored! Quickly—make me something marvelous!"

He made her a silver pitcher that could fly from guest to guest, pouring wine into their cups and never allowing itself to get empty. Pasiphae was pleased. Now she knew her banquets could progress even if the serving maids were being flogged.

At this time, Minos had begun to plan a series of campaigns against other island states of the Middle Sea. He asked Daedalus to do what he could to improve the quality of his war fleet. Within a year Daedalus had replaced the great clumsy sternsman's oar with a pivoting steering board called a rudder, and had also devised a sliding bench for the rowers. These improvements made the ships of Crete swifter and more maneuverable by far than any that had ever sailed the waters of the world.

Minos was more than pleased. He couldn't praise Daedalus enough and heaped so many gifts on him that the old man was bewildered; he already had more than he could use. Nevertheless, Daedalus was fully aware of how important it was to have earned the esteem of an all-powerful ruler like Minos.

It was at this point, at the very flower of the old craftsman's career, that he fell into deadly peril. The image of Pasiphae had begun to scorch his sleep, and he realized that he would have to do something about it.

He took a lump of pure crystal and wrought a special mirror, which he laid on the altar in the temple of Aphrodite. He hoped the goddess might be pleased because, viewing herself in this wondrous glass while combing her long yellow hair, she would be able to see the back of her head.

That night Aphrodite appeared to him. "Thank you for your gift," she said.

"Beautiful goddess, you are more than welcome."

"Now, what is it you wish of me?"

"Are you sure I want something?"

"In my experience, mortals do not make gifts to gods without expecting much in return. What is it you wish?"

"I'm desperately in love with Queen Pasiphae and need your help," said Daedalus.

"Tell me, how long do you think you'd last if Minos knew you were trying to take his wife?"

"Oh, Goddess, if she returned my love I'd be so filled with creative energy, with such brilliant inventiveness that I'd be able to surmount all difficulties."

"It's hard to be brilliant without a head. And your venerable pate, my friend, would be whisked off your shoulders by the king's executioners before you could kiss Pasiphae twice. Besides, it's ridiculous. You're much too old for her."

"I thought you could arrange anything in the love line, no matter how ridiculous."

"I can. I can. As a matter of fact, I'm planning something truly grotesque for that Pasiphae of yours. She's a boastful, sacrilegious slut and I've always disliked her."

"Aphrodite, please. . . . I have asked you to help me, and you offer a disservice."

"I haven't forgotten the mirror you made me. Find yourself another girl and I'll send her your way no matter how young and beautiful she is. But take my advice and keep away from Pasiphae. Dreadful things are in store for her and bad luck is contagious."

With this, she vanished.

The next morning Pasiphae was strolling in the paddock when a bull ambled her way, the largest and most splendid animal she had ever seen. This was no bull of the Minos herd, but a prize stud belonging to Helios, the Sun's Charioteer, whose golden suncattle were the envy of all the gods.

Aphrodite had borrowed the animal for her own purposes, coaxing the miserly Helios to lend him out. The bull's hide was a hot, dazzling gold, and his eyes were pools of amber light. His hooves and long, sharp horns were of polished ivory, and he snorted joyously through coral-pink nostrils.

As soon as Pasiphae saw him, she felt herself strangling with passion. She fell violently, monstrously, permanently in love with the bull.

She went to Daedalus and told him. He listened quietly as she told her tale; by the end of it, she was sobbing. He stroked her arm timidly and trembled at the touch.

"Do not fret, beautiful queen," he said. "No living creature can possibly resist you—god, man, or beast."

"Please don't flatter me. This is tearing me to pieces. I know that bull has a loving heart. One look into those golden eyes and I understood him to the depths of his sweet, straightforward soul. But how can he possibly return my feelings? I'm sure he must prefer his own kind. I'm going to kill myself."

"No, Pasiphae. Don't despair. I'll help you."

"How?"

"I've thought of a way."

"If you can do anything, old friend, I'll be eternally grateful."

Daedalus went to work. He fashioned an exquisite wooden cow, hollowing it out so that Pasiphae could comfortably position herself inside. It had amber eyes, ivory horns, and ivory hooves with wheels in the hooves and springs in the wheels. As a last touch, he tenderly upholstered his wooden heifer in pliant calfskin and painted the entire piece so artfully that it seemed to have a hide of dappled moonlight.

After finishing the cow, he began to peg another frame together. His son, Icarus, who was also his apprentice and a formidably bright lad, was watching him all this while. He knew why his father had made the wooden cow, but he didn't understand what he was doing now. However, when the youth saw the frame taking shape under his father's incredibly swift carpentry, he began to understand.

"Don't tell me you're making a wooden bull," he said.

"You see that I am."

"Yes. I see that it will be a wooden bull to match the wooden cow. What I can't believe is that you're actually doing it."

"Please, Icarus . . ."

"I can't believe that a man so intelligent would do something so stupid, so fatally stupid."

"Please, son . . . don't sit in judgment of me. Not today. I'm under a terrible strain."

"You'll feel worse when you're under the ax."

"You don't understand," said Daedalus. "You've never been in love."

"Well, if love can turn a brain into porridge, I want no part of it. Are you actually going to cram yourself into that thing and court Pasiphae?"

"That's the idea. I'll take her on any terms, son. Any at all."

Icarus stormed out of the workshop. He was furious. And terrified for his father. He hurried to the temple of Aphrodite and knelt at the altar to pray.

"Oh, Goddess, you who preside over that bewildering state called love and who, therefore, I presume, must have a loving heart yourself—hear me, I pray. This passion you wield has addled the most brilliant mind on earth. Retrieve him, I beseech, from this matchless folly. For the sake of all of us who will find our lives enriched by inventions still unhatched in that fertile brain, please save my father from his desperate ploy. Dissuade him from secreting himself inside a wooden bull to court the contents of a wooden cow, and to court death under the double ax."

Aphrodite looked down from Mount Olympus and saw the young man at her altar. She was struck by his appearance. He was altogether elegant, a cleanly made youth, his eyes aflame with intelligence. When prayed to, the goddess seldom paid heed to what was being said, but based her decision on whether or not she liked the looks of whoever was doing the praying. And she liked this young man very much. Aphrodite came down from the mountain of the gods and hovered invisibly over the workshop where Daedalus was finishing his wooden bull. The old man suddenly found himself unable to breathe; he was choking on sawdust. He rushed outside, panting, and hurried down to the meadow. It was midafternoon. The sun was pressing close, making heat waves dance, turning the meadow into a rippling green lake.

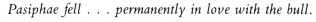

Pasiphae fell . . . permanently in love with the bull.

*Daedalus fashioned an exquisite wooden cow, hollowing it out
so that Pasiphae could comfortably position herself inside.*

Crossing the lake was a golden galleon. Daedalus blinked
and rubbed his eyes. He couldn't believe what he was seeing. In
the blur of brightness, a ship drifted and burned. It became a bit
of the sun itself, melting and congealing on the grass. Then his
vision cleared. A golden bull came ambling toward him. At the
sight of this magnificent animal, his heart shriveled within him.
He realized how shabby, how futile his wooden bull would seem
to Pasiphae, who had looked upon this throbbing mountain of
hot blood, this golden beast.

How could he have hoped that she would be deceived? Icarus was right. He was no lover . . . no longer an artisan even, for if his judgment were failing then his hands must surely follow. Splendor had gone. And hope. He was a poor, enfeebled, crazed old man whose plain duty was to go back to his workshop, take his sharpest knife, and cut his own throat, claiming a place in Hades while his deeds were still being hailed on earth. The mad queen could have her wooden cow and her unspeakable rendezvous.

That night, as the moon was rising, the great golden bull saw the form of a graceful cow gliding toward him over the meadow, mooing musically. He bugled softly in return, swished his ropy tail, and pawed the earth. By the end of the evening, Pasiphae was very happy. And the next night she thought she would burst with joy as she rolled into the meadow, peering through the eyeholes of the wooden cow. For the same molten moon hung low in the sky, and very soon, she knew, her bull would come to her.

The moon climbed and paled, and no bull came. She tried calling him, mooing musically as she had the night before, but heard only her own thin, scratchy voice. Suddenly, she hated her voice, hated everything about herself, loathed her entire human condition.

The bull did not come to her that night. Nor the night after. Nor the night after that. Every night she fitted herself into the wooden cow, and rolled into the meadow and waited. Every dawn she departed.

Then, one night, she found she could no longer fit into the wooden frame and knew why. Some months later, she gave birth to a child, half boy, half bull-calf. Pasiphae refused to name her son, but as rumors spread, the populace dubbed him Minotaur, or Minos's Bull.

5

The New Monster

inos was very much disturbed by these rumors and the gossip of the populace. He summoned Daedalus and said, "I have a different kind of project for you—one that will serve me against domestic enemies as your weapons have served me against the foreign foe. I want you to design and build a kind of puzzle-garden, a maze so cunningly wrought that no prisoner will be able to find a way out. Make it big; it will house many guests of the state as they await their turn with my busy executioners. Start immediately. You may have a thousand slaves."

Daedalus designed a maze and supervised its construction. It was a marvel. Its walls were tall, impenetrable, thorny hedges. It was full of blind lanes, lanes that angled, circled, doubled back on themselves, and trailed off into nowhere. When the work was done, Daedalus reported to the king, whom he had not seen for six months. Minos toured the maze, which he named the Labyrinth or Ax-Garden.

"You have done your usual fine job," said Minos, "and I mean to reward you."

"Pleasing you is reward enough," said Daedalus, who detected something in the king's manner that filled him with terror.

"Permit me to differ," said Minos. "I know your modest, undemanding nature, but I can't allow myself to take advantage of it. Now hear me. You shall immediately move your workshop into this Labyrinth amd attach such dwelling quarters as you require. You shall take your son and your servants too. In other words, loyal friend, this beautiful puzzle-garden shall be your home from now on."

"You mean I am to be the first prisoner in your maze?"

"You, a prisoner?" cried Minos. "How absurd! I'm only trying to please you. I know you like to be surrounded by your own artifacts. And here I am putting you in the middle of your greatest construction—and giving it to you on a lifelong lease. And mind you, in the exclusive residential area, not the prisoners' quarters."

"Oh, how touching," continued Minos. "You're weeping tears of pure gratitude, aren't you, old fellow? And yet, so foul is human nature that there are those who actually tell me that you're the most ungrateful of mortals. Can you credit such wickedness?"

Daedalus started to say something, but Minos stopped him.

"No . . . no, not a word of thanks, please! I haven't finished describing the benefits to be heaped upon you. For you shall have interesting neighbors: the ex-queen Pasiphae and her son—a most unusual youngster, I'm told. Well, I'm off now, Daedalus. We're sailing against Athens. It may be a lengthy campaign, but I can leave with my mind at rest, knowing that I have fully repaid my old artisan for his matchless service to me and my family."

Living in the maze, Daedalus saw Pasiphae every day but never spoke to her. Nor did she speak to him, or even seem to know that he was there. She was aware of nothing but her horned child, whom she cared for tenderly. She was never heard speaking to him, only singing a crooning, wordless song.

When the child was barely six months old, he was the size of a twelve-year-old boy, but much more muscular. His rippling torso was covered with dense golden fur and his horns were ivory knives growing into ivory spears. The boy's face was rather squashed, with upturned coral nostrils and huge brimming eyes like pools of molten gold. He trotted after his mother wherever she went.

At this time, Daedalus never sought to leave the Labyrinth. Through sheer inventiveness he had refined its grid work of paths, shifting them into new patterns every day. But he had also made a spool that rolled through the twisting lanes, heading inexorably toward the exit, unreeling its thread as it went, so that whoever held the other end could leave the Labyrinth by the quickest route.

His only visitor from outside was the princess Ariadne, and he suspected that she came only to claim the dolls he kept making for her and that she never outgrew.

"But," he thought, "greed can imitate love too, as long as I can satisfy it. And I do care for the selfish child as much as I can care for anyone now."

One day, when Ariadne came to him with a sullen face because she had lost her way and wandered for hours, he gave her the pathfinding spool and taught her how to use it. He didn't need it for himself any more. The shifting grid of the maze was stamped on his brain now.

Pasiphae turned to eating. . . . One day she simply burst. . . . The ground where she had stood looked like the floor of a slaughterhouse.

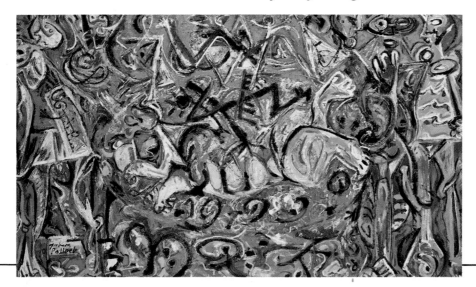

Minotauromachy (1935) by Pablo Picasso

*The Minotaur's anger swelled into unfocused hatred
and became pure murder seeking occasion.*

Pasiphae, like many women misled by the Love Goddess, turned to eating. She kept trying to stuff food into her aching emptiness, but the more she ate, the emptier she felt. She was a tall woman, so her face went first, blurring and then ballooning. Then her body bloated. She grew a gut, then a paunch. Her legs became quivering blobs, her arms two gelatinous bolsters.

One day she simply burst. She had devoured an entire shoulder of ox and washed it down with a half barrel of wine. She burst with the dipper still at her lips, exploding into gobs of flesh. The ground where she had stood looked like the floor of a slaughterhouse.

Her son watched all this. He was the size of a half-grown bull-calf now and was growing fast. But his brimming golden eyes still seemed too large for his head. Bewildered, he ran in circles, bawling, searching for his mother. When he realized that she was gone, that the bloody offal littering the grass was all that was left of her warmth, her fragrance, her singing voice, a puzzled rage began to work on him. His anger swelled into unfocused hatred and became pure murder seeking occasion.

He grew now with monstrous speed, and in three days had reached his full size. The Minotaur stood ten feet tall, had long, needle-pointed ivory horns and a set of razor-sharp hooves, and was as powerful as a wild bull. But he had the wits of a man, the brooding, vengeful nature of man, and a pair of huge hands that closed into fists of bone.

He began to prowl the lanes of the Labyrinth, looking for something to kill. He entered a holding area where prisoners were kept, awaiting the return of Minos, who would pass final sentence upon them. They were to wait no longer. As soon as the Minotaur saw them—they were the first living creatures he had seen since the death of his mother—he charged. Before they understood what the hurtling figure was, it was goring them with its sharp horns, lifting them into the air, and hurling them into the thorn hedge, where they hung dying. Others were knocked to the ground as the monster charged. He turned then and trampled them into bloody rags.

Those who were still alive after the first charge scattered and fled. But the Minotaur's rage was a separate organism, nourished by blood, growing with every murder. He snorted and bellowed down the lanes, pursuing the survivors, hunting them down systematically and cornering them in blind lanes. He gored them, trampled them, and battered them to death with his fists. By the end of the long afternoon, when the last bloody light was fading from the hedge tops, he had killed every one.

Among the corpses were a few of Daedalus's smithy slaves, for the old man had sent a party out to see what the screaming meant. Only two of them returned, both badly gored, and they gasped out their tale. Daedalus immediately closed the hedge gaps, encircling his area with a single wall so thick and thorny that not even the Minotaur could break through. He also sealed all the gaps in the outer wall of the Labyrinth, penning the monster in.

Minotaure (1933) by Pablo Picasso

6

The Tribute

The ships of Minos went off to battle and they swept the Athenian fleet off the sea, forcing Athens to surrender. The young Theseus watched the battle from a hilltop. His heart grew sick within him as he saw what was happening. The long, brass-prowed Cretan ships fell upon the slower Athenian vessels like hawks among pigeons. Theseus watched his father's ships being grappled and boarded, saw double-bladed axes flash in the sun and the sea redden with Athenian blood. The Cretans did not even bother to board some of the enemy ships but simply rammed them, driving brass prows into wooden hulls. Their archers stood on deck and calmly sent arrows into the Athenian seamen who had leapt overboard. Those who tried to swim were gaffed like fish.

Aegeus was forced to surrender and accept the terms imposed by Minos. Every year, on the first day of the Spring Sowing, twenty of the strongest and most handsome young men of Athens and twenty of the healthiest, most beautiful maidens were to be sent to Crete to enter the slave pens of Minos. But not as ordinary slaves. They were to be trained as bull dancers for a year and the next year sent into the arena against the wild bulls of the Minos herd.

Their deaths would be useful and not without honor, Minos proclaimed. After all, when the bulls had finished with them, they would be buried in the wheat fields, where their bodies would fatten the crops.

Theseus had sneaked into the council room, where the terms of surrender were being dictated. No one saw him; he had blended in with the shadows and stood very still, listening. He studied

the cold, pinched face of Minos, who was black-cloaked and wore no ornament except a spiked iron crown, as if to emphasize his role as pirate king. And the lad saw how that runty figure breathed power, and how crushed and humiliated Aegeus looked as he accepted the terms of his defeat. Bitterly the boy learned how fortune alters physique, how victors grow and losers shrink.

Then and there Theseus vowed to himself that he would be among those sent to Crete and that he would fight the wild

Forty of the best young Athenians were taken to Crete, where they died dancing in the arena.

bulls and the ax men on their own territory. He told himself that one day he would stand in the throne room at Knossos, dictating terms of surrender to this same Minos . . . or be buried in the wheat field, as losers deserve.

Two springs passed. Forty of the best young Athenians were taken to Crete, where they died dancing in the arena and were planted in the ploughed fields. Then the rite was changed. One day Minos was informed that Pasiphae's crossbreed child had grown into a fearsome monster and had slaughtered the prisoners in the Labyrinth. All Crete was abuzz with tales of the beast. This pleased Minos tremendously. The monster, once a source of shame to him, now offered a rich opportunity to spread

The blood of Athenian youth would dung the roots of royal prestige and make the name of Minoan Crete shine darkly forever.

Burial (1943) by Bradley Walker Tomlin

46

the name of Minos into every corner of every island in the Middle Sea and to charge that name with horror.

This was exactly what he wanted—for the mere sound of his name to strike terror into the hearts of everyone, to have the mere sight of a Cretan ship or a Cretan chariot freeze an enemy with fear, making him flutter helplessly as a dove before a diving hawk.

The Minotaur, who had just enjoyed its first orgy of murder in the maze, would now serve the king. It would not lack for victims. There were still those suspected of treason. Or, if not of treason exactly, of dissent. Or, if not quite of dissent, then of insufficiently enthusiastic approval of everything Minos did, had done, and would do. In other words, there were still those whom Minos disliked, and this was enough to qualify them for residence in the Labyrinth and the attentions of the Minotaur.

Still, domestic victims were not the big issue. They were only something for the Minotaur to practice on. It would be upon the occasion of the next Spring Sowing, when again the flower of Athenian youth would be brought as sacrificial tributes to Knossos, that the monster could be most profitably employed. The Minotaur would replace the ordinary wild bulls and go into the arena against the beautiful young people. Their blood would dung the roots of royal prestige and make the name of Minoan Crete shine darkly forever.

The king's daughters drank in the rumors. The word *Athens* held a special resonance for them. It was Theseus, a young prince of that land, whose name had been sung by the bones. By twisting ways, then, the Hag's prophecy was coming true. Theseus would come to Crete. Once there, he could be persuaded to change his destiny from victim to husband.

Ariadne, of course, did not know that her sister had been promised a share in this fiancé, and Phaedra was careful to keep her secret. Being very much Minos's daughter, she had begun spinning plans of her own.

7

Theseus Embarks

When the third spring rolled around, Theseus was ready to go to Crete, but not as a sacrifice. During the past year he had prepared himself for mortal combat by roaming the dangerous parts of the Hellenic Peninsula posing as a harmless traveler with a heavy purse. He had invited the notice of the most savage bandits who infested the mountain roads, had been bushwacked many times and sliced and battered, but was young enough to heal rapidly, especially while enjoying himself so.

Theseus had learned much from his journey through the mountains. "This I now know," he said to himself. "To learn about your enemy before the fight, not during it; never to accept his terms of combat, but to impose your own; and, above all, to avoid doing what he expects. The key to victory is surprise, surprise, surprise . . . especially when your foe is bigger, which he always is."

So it was that when the next spring tribute came, Theseus did not sail to Crete with the other young Athenians. He went to the port at Piraeus in the garb of an apprentice seaman, and

Theseus shipped aboard a merchant vessel bound for
the southern islands of the Middle Sea. . . . One dawn
he leaped overboard and swam ashore.

he shipped aboard a merchant vessel bound for the southern
islands of the Middle Sea. He did not mean to stay with the ship.
His intention was to sail with it until it reached Cretan waters,
then dive overboard and swim ashore. Once there, he would pose
as a shipwrecked sailor from a land other than Athens and scout
around Knossos, learning as much as possible about Minos and
the Minotaur.

That same night, Minos, who after a string of victories was
sleeping more or less dreamlessly, had his rest broken—not by
the livid pictures of a dream, but by a voice speaking out of the
darkness. It was a soft, melodic voice, but full of authority:

> It creeps ashore, the danger.
> Your land to be cursed,
> maddened by thirst.
> Beware the stranger.
>
> When you have passed away,
> Crete will be ruled
> by a castaway.
>
> Burning sky,
> fountains dry.
> Take care,
> Beware
> the castaway.

Minos took the voice very seriously. He issued orders to
his coastal troops to keep close watch and seize any shipwrecked
sailors who came ashore.

"Be vigilant," he told his captain. "I have learned that spies,
very dangerous ones, are attempting to sneak ashore and probe
our defenses. If a single one gets past the beaches, the company
patrolling the area can report to the Minotaur."

One dawn, Theseus leaped overboard and swam toward a
land dimly hulking on the horizon. Threading his way among

rocks with the fluid skill of someone spawned by the sea, he made his way to the beach and waded ashore. He lifted his face to the kindling sky and said: "Thank you, whoever you are, wherever you are, for bringing me this far."

Then he turned to the sea and spoke: "Oh, Lord, who is supposed to be my father, if you really did steal my mother from her husband, you can repay us both by helping me now. I cannot tell you exactly what I want, but with such vast oceanic powers as yours, you should be able to do something."

Now Poseidon was good-natured when not offended and had always been entertained by this smallest and most combative of his sons. However, he was used to doing things in a big, gusty way and had no mind for detail. Those he wished to reward, he heaped with gifts of pearl and galleons full of sunken gold. When he wished to punish, he sent drought or tidal wave. Hearing his son's prayer, then, he decided to withhold his waters from the thirsty spring sky over Crete. And no rain fell.

Theseus turned from the sea and began his journey inland. But he didn't get far. Almost immediately, he was intercepted by a squad of armored men who wordlessly knocked him over the head with their spear shafts, bound his unconscious body to a mule, and took him to Knossos.

8

The Castaway

Theseus was shackled to an iron ring set in rock, and left in the stinking darkness of the smallest cell in the dungeon system forming the cellars of the Ax-House. The cell was so loathsome that he rejoiced when the guards came for him, thinking that he would now be led out to execution, and hoping only that he would not be tortured first. Instead, he was led up a marble stairway to an enormous sunny chamber, where a little man sat on a throne of ivory and gold. The captain of the guard prostrated himself, wriggled forward, and kissed the king's sandal. A soldier rammed the haft of his ax between Theseus's shoulders, pressing him to the tiled floor. He lay prone, hoping he was not expected to kiss the royal foot himself. With his face against the floor, he heard the rattle of arms and the shuffle of boots as the guards departed.

"Arise," said a voice.

He arose and faced the throne. It was a warm day, but the king wore a robe of Egyptian weave called byssus, dyed purple and embroidered with the double-ax in heavy gold thread. Trying to forget his stinking rags, Theseus stood tall as he could and waited for the king to speak.

"You are a spy, of course."

Theseus shuddered when he heard the little man's thunderous voice.

"No, Your Majesty."

There was a silence. Theseus stood with his head bowed, but he knew the king was studying him. He raised his head and looked into the king's eyes, then looked away again. Minos's eyes were flat black disks. They rotated slowly on their axes. Theseus could not bear their gaze.

"Prisoners are not ordinarily questioned by the king, you know."

"I am grateful for the honor, Your Majesty."

"Do you know what happens to spies in Crete?"

"I repeat, my lord, I am no spy, but a shipwrecked seaman."

"A castaway?"

"Yes, sire. A castaway."

"However you describe yourself, I think you came to spy. The penalties for that are severe."

"For the third time, I am no spy."

"Why did you come to Crete?"

"Not by intention, sire. I was shipwrecked."

"No vessel has foundered recently in these waters. I am kept informed of such matters."

"It was a Mycenaean trading vessel. It broke up on a reef about ten miles offshore. I caught a spar and drifted in."

"You're not a very skillful liar."

"I lack practice. I'm accustomed to telling the truth."

"Be careful, now. Every additional lie will cost you several hours of agony. Have you never served as an officer aboard a foreign galley docked at Knossos?"

"No."

"Perhaps you served as a member of the crew, concealing your station, as a spy would."

"I swear by all the gods that I have never before set foot

The guards returned Theseus to his cell and shackled him.

on Crete. I am a voyager, true. I have traveled much, but never to Crete."

"Well, you have made your last landfall, voyager."

"So it seems . . . and I wish it had been in any other place than this miserable slaughterhouse of an island."

"Are you trying to act demented to escape the penalties of the law? It won't help you, you know. Maniacs who commit crimes here are simply considered crazy criminals. They receive no privilege denied to sanity."

"Hear me, Minos," said Theseus. "You have the power to order my death. Then do so. I had rather perish under the double-ax than be bored to death by your dreary, malevolent tirade. Young though I am, I have met *real* killers—evil men, to be sure, but brave—who did their own killing. And I am not to be intimidated by a poisonous little toad who happens to wear a crown."

Theseus broke off. The king had toppled from his throne. He writhed on the floor uttering broken shouts. Foam flecked his mouth. Guards rushed in. The king arched and spat and beat the back of his head on the floor. The captain of the guard knelt to take the king in his arms. His men had surrounded Theseus with drawn swords, hiding Minos from view. But Theseus heard his strangled shout break into words: "Don't kill him . . . don't kill him."

They returned Theseus to his cell and shackled him. He lay on the straw listening to the rats. "I'm sorry he spared me," he said to himself. "I'd rather be dead than rot in this filthy hole."

He prayed to Poseidon then, very fervently, but received no answer. A rat came while he slept and bit off half his ear. He hoped to bleed to death then, and tried to encourage the bleeding by digging at his wound, but the pain was too intense. "No use torturing myself," he thought. "I'll leave it to the experts." He fell asleep again, and by morning the bleeding had stopped. The wound festered. He tossed and burned.

When the girl appeared, he thought she was fledged by his fever and waited for her to disappear. But she did not. Was she another joke of the capricious gods? He shook his head trying to rid himself of the vision, but he couldn't shake her away. Her eyes were burning holes in the murk. She had ivory-brown legs, cascading black hair, a curly mouth. He dragged himself to his hands and knees and faced her with his head raised. She did not disappear. She stood there silently, her dainty white feet spurning the dirty straw. She was dressed in court fashion—in a long, full skirt, and naked above the waist save for the drape of her shining hair. The girl was small and slender, not yet nubile.

"Who are you?" he whispered.

"I am Ariadne."

"I greet you, lovely maiden, whoever you are."

"I just told you who I was," said Ariadne. "What did you do to my father?"

"Have I the honor of knowing your father?"

"He's the king. You threw him into a fit. He'll never forgive you."

"I had nothing to do with his fit."

"He says you're some kind of wicked sorcerer, employed by his enemies. He's going to do dreadful things to you, unless you vanish or something. Can you do that?"

"Not without help."

"In your opinion, am I marriageable?"

"Well . . . perhaps not quite yet," said Theseus.

"Almost?"

"You'll be very lovely when you do grow up."

"How can you tell about what you can't see?"

"Because what I can see is beautiful, and the rest of you will surely match."

"Good-bye now."

"Don't go," said Theseus.

"I'll be back."

Darkness swarmed. Red pain flared.

She was back. Taller, long-legged, coltish—an ivory wand of a maiden, the coolest, cleanest thing he had ever seen. She smelled like the snow-freighted wind blowing off the mountains of Greece. She stood erect, smiling.

"Well, am I grown up?"

"By the gods, I don't believe it! How long have I been here?"

"Little girls grow up fast."

He lay back on the straw. A wave of sickness broke over him.

"What's wrong with you?"

"Nothing much. I'm probably dying."

"So soon? We have prisoners who've been here for twenty years—some of them without hands or feet because the rats ate them off."

"Why don't you run along, Princess? It can't be pleasant for you here."

"It stinks, if that's what you mean. But a lot of interesting things do."

She knelt swiftly and touched his ear. He jerked his head away.

"What happened to it?" asked Ariadne.

"One of those rats you were talking about."

"It looks dreadful. Say a spell and make it grow again."

"I'm no sorcerer, I told you. Please now, be on your way."

She knelt on the straw. Her ivory knee almost touched his face. He felt himself reviving in the piny fragrance of her young body. She seemed to cleanse the foul vapors. He pulled himself up to a sitting position.

"I know who you are," she said. "You're Theseus, Prince of Athens."

"Nonsense! Princes aren't found in prisons."

"That's where you're wrong. Most prisoners here are of very good family. So tell me the truth."

"Why is it important to you who I am?"

"Because I'm destined to marry Theseus, Prince of Athens."

"Has he asked you?"

"Wouldn't you remember if you had? I'm destined to marry you, and you're destined to marry me."

"How did you learn of this destiny?"

"From a reliable witch. A very magical one. She gathered bones from the killing ground in the maze and hung them on the western slope of a hill where the wind blows. The bones danced and sang. They sang:

> Tigers are wild,
> dogs are tame.
> Listen, dear child,
> to your husband's name.
>
> Theseus, Theseus
> A prince for a princess,
> Theseus is his name.
>
> Roses are red,
> wounds are too.
> Him you shall wed,
> I tell you true.

"Anyone would be happy to marry you," whispered Theseus. "You're exquisitely pretty. And smell marvelous. And sing like a lark."

"You sound like a man who wants to kiss me."

"You're so lovely and clean. And I'm in so foul a state. How can I touch you?"

"I'll take a bath when I leave. I'll have to anyway."

"Look, they're ready to kill me just for being cast away on this island. What would they do to me for fondling the king's daughter?"

"Oh, they'd whisk you to the chopping block and lop your head off."

"Exactly."

"Unless sorcerers can grow their heads back—as lizards do their tails."

"You have some useful ideas about magic," said Theseus.

"That witch taught me a few things."

"Show me."

"Not here. I need some stuff. Frog . . . cat . . . fire of thorns. An alder stick and a bag of corn . . ."

"Sing that again," he was surprised to hear himself whispering.

"I wasn't singing."

Pain flowed from his mangled earlobe and coursed like lava through his head. He groaned and fell back on the straw.

He heard her singing:

> Thorn and thistle,
> gristle grue.
> When I whistle,
> it means *you!*

He tried to speak but could not. She whistled. He saw the straw heave beside his face. He couldn't move away. Out slithered a rat, an enormous gray one with faint black markings. It held something pale in its mouth and danced toward the girl like a poodle. She held out her hand and the rat leaped up. Balancing itself on her palm, it offered the ear. She took it and kissed the rat on the head. It disappeared.

Ariadne turned the ear, studying it. She spat on the raw edge and smoothed it out with her little finger, then knelt to Theseus and pressed it in place. It was like a piece of ice; it froze the fire in his head. Pain drained deliciously out. He felt the ear; it was whole. He looked at her. She smiled. And, very gently, he kissed her curly mouth.

"You're getting politer," she whispered. "Anything else I can fix?"

He drew away. "Just talk to me."

"Talk?"

"Yes, it's a way of touching too."

"Maybe you *are* old under that beard."

"Nobody's that old, Princess. If you were to walk past an Egyptian tomb, the mummies would jump out and run after you."

"Oh, gruesome! . . . Someone told me about those tombs once. They're very tall and full of cats. An Egyptian told me."

"Where did you meet him?"

"He put into port one day in a big boat made of paper or cloth or something. Big, clumsy things, hardly like a boat at all. . . . Egyptians are weird. They look like long, rusty knives. Reddish brown, you know, with stilt legs and bird faces. But he was nice. He told me all about cats and tombs and the moon eating the sun. Egyptians are very religious—worse than us."

Her hand lay on the straw beside him. He studied it as he drank in the clear, beautifully articulated stream of words. It was a childish hand still, the fingers very long. He put his hand over it. It moved in his grasp like a little bird. Tears scalded his eyes.

"What's the matter?"

"Nothing. Tell me more things. Tell me about your mother."

"What about her?"

"There's a curious tale—that she eloped with a bull and had a child, half man, half bull . . ."

Her eyes were black disks like her father's, but larger and more brilliant. Slowly, they began to spin.

62

"I can't talk about that," said Ariadne.

"Why not?"

"It's a family secret. And in our family that's a state secret. You know what happens to anyone who tells? They get their tongues torn out with hot pincers."

"You can tell me. I won't tell your father."

"Why should I tell you anything? You won't even admit who you are. But I know. You're Theseus, Theseus, Theseus. . . ."

She brought her face to his. Her eyes were black disks like her father's, but larger and more brilliant. Slowly, they began to spin. "Aren't you? Aren't you?"

"Yes, . . ." he murmured.

Ariadne laughed. Her eyes spun faster. Blackness spun inside his head, flowed out, and engulfed him.

9

The Sacrifice

he king was closeted with his daughter.

"Well," he said. "I have indulged your whim and allowed you to visit his cell."

"It wasn't a whim," said Ariadne. "I was trying to help you."

"Did you learn any more than I did?"

"He confuses me."

"Is he a wizard?"

"Too young. Much too young. I think he's what he says he is—a castaway. Why should you doubt it? Many shipwrecked sailors are washed up on our shores. They've never bothered you. You just pop them into the slave-pen."

"Not this one," said Minos.

"Why?"

"Something spoke to me in the night, warning me against a castaway and against drought. This fellow appears, and it stops raining. It hasn't rained for weeks, not a drop. The streams are dry. Crops are withering in the fields."

"What are you going to do, kill him?"

"Not yet. I want to know his secret. He shall be tortured until he talks."

Phaedra stood before her abductor. She examined him from the bottom of his hooves to the tips of his horns. He was huge.

"Father, he won't survive a minute of torture. He's too weak."

"Are you sure he's not pretending?"

"If you want to torture him long enough to learn anything, you'd better shift him out of that cell. The rats almost ate his ear off. At this rate, he won't last three days."

"You're suggesting that I turn him loose?"

"Not at all. Simply put him in the Labyrinth until he gets his health back and is able to bear a touch or two of the hot iron without dying."

"I'll think about it. Return now to the temple. Dance with your priestesses and pray for rain."

Since Phaedra had learned that her sister was visiting the castaway, she followed Ariadne everywhere. There is no instinct surer than jealousy—especially when your rival is your sister—and Phaedra had immediately sensed that this stranger was Theseus. She felt helpless. Ariadne had already begun to blossom, especially since the stranger had come, but she, Phaedra, was still a little girl. She examined herself very carefully in a mirror and saw nothing to interest anyone. But if she wasn't ready for Theseus herself, no one else would have him either, especially not Ariadne.

And now things were worse. The prisoner had been transferred to the Labyrinth, which was a dreadful development. For Ariadne, armed with that damned spool Daedalus had given her, could slither in and out of the maze like a hedge-snake.

On this night, Phaedra had followed her sister to the temple of the Horned Moon and perched herself on the outer stone wall. The vestals came out and began to dance. Phaedra hummed wordlessly along with the flutes. The moon was hot and white, and shadows danced among the vestals. One shadow thickened and flowed toward Phaedra. A hand clutched her with enormous strength.

The King Playing with the Queen (1944) by Max Ernst

She felt herself being lifted high over a shoulder and borne away with great speed. A heavy arm pressed against the back of her thighs, holding her close. Her head swung against a downy back, rolling with muscle. She was in a swoon of speed, a daze of helplessness, and wanting the ride to go on and on.

Suddenly it was over. She was swung down and set on her feet. Phaedra stood before her abductor. She examined him from the bottom of his hooves to the tip of his horns. He was huge. A dense pelt of golden hair covered his shoulders, chest, belly, and thighs. He looked all golden in the moonlight. His horns glittered, and his eyes were pools of light.

"Hello, Minotaur," she said.

He grunted.

"Are you going to kill me?"

"No."

"Why did you carry me off, then?"

"I heard you singing. Your voice . . ." he reached out and touched her lips with the tip of a hard finger.

"What about my voice?"

"My mother used to sing to me. Then, one day, she was in pieces on the ground. Your voice is like hers."

"Well, she was my mother too."

"Yours?"

"I'm your sister—half anyway. The one called Phaedra."

He didn't answer. She was frightened by the silence. His eyes were burning. Finally he spoke.

"You'll stay with me now."

"Will I?"

"I want you to."

"Suppose I don't want to?" she said.

"Once you try it, you will."

"Try what, exactly?"

"Living with me. Doing what I do."

"But you're a monster. I'm not."

"You can be anything you like. Look at our mother. She got herself up as a cow to catch my father. And that old wizard who helped her can help you. He'll make you some sharp horns and a pair of razor-hooves, and you'll be able to run the maze with me and have fun with prisoners."

"What kind of fun?"

"Wild, screechy fun, the kind girls like. Goring with your horns, trampling with your hooves. You'll love it."

"The oracles say . . .
that the drought has been caused
by a stranger in our midst."

"I'm not so sure."

"Of course you will. You're my sister, you say."

"Only half."

"That's plenty. We have the same crazy mother. And your demon father makes mine look like a bleating calf."

"I can't stay with you, but I'll come visiting," she said.

"Every day?"

"Well . . ."

"If you don't, I'll come get you."

"Almost every day. . . . Tell me, do you eat all these people you kill?"

"I don't eat people. That's a myth. I just kill them; the vultures pick their bones. What I eat is grass and things."

"Grass? I can't eat that."

"Sing something."

"Then will you let me go?"

"If you want me to. But I can always come and get you again. And I will—again and again, until you decide you might as well stay."

"Hush if you want me to sing."

Ariadne was told that the king wished to see her. She hastened to him. He told her that the stranger was to be given to ritual slaughter.

"I suppose it's necessary, if you say so."

"The oracles say so. They state that the drought has been caused by a stranger in our midst. And the populace, always ready to relieve its fears with simple answers, has accepted the idea that the castaway is accursed. He comes here, and crops wither in the field. Cattle die; men and women are dying. They believe that only his ritual dismemberment will appease the gods and bring rain."

"But is that what you believe, Father?"

"I believe the lad is unlucky, for he is to die young. I believe in the drought and the suffering of our people, and their rage and fear. They believe in gods, curses, and oracles, and I welcome such faith. Absolute belief feeds absolute authority. I shall decree the performance of the people's will. You priestesses shall howl your prayers, the bull dancers will perform, and the boy will be given to the Minotaur."

"And then—suppose it doesn't rain?"

"It will rain, or it will not. If not, I shall detect a flaw in the ritual. The oracles will find another victim. I shall certify his guilt; you will dance again; he will be given to the Minotaur, then dismembered. And so on. It has to rain sometime."

Ariadne knelt before her father. "As usual, sire, your wisdom leaves me speechless with admiration."

"One more thing," said Minos. "I mean you to play a key role in this ceremony. When the bull dancers have finished, you will appear as your ancestress, Europa, being abducted by Zeus in the form of a bull. And that bull shall be the best in all our herds, of tremendous size, unblemished whiteness, and fiery spirit. Following that, the stranger will be brought into the ring and given to the Minotaur. And the drama of what will happen then will divert our poor drought victims, even if it doesn't bring rain."

Ariadne visited Theseus in the maze and told him what her father had decreed. He laughed.

"What's so funny about the Minotaur? I only hope you find him that amusing when he comes at you in the ring."

"No use weeping beforehand."

"You have guts, I'll say that for you. Anyone else would be scared witless."

"You haven't met many heroes. It's well known we have more guts than wits. Actually, I'm not entirely like that. I have sharp wits and not quite enough courage."

Ariadne stared at him, then reached into her tunic and pulled out a spool. "Watch," she said. She tossed the spool onto the ground. It darted through the hedge, out of sight, unreeling itself as it went and leaving one end of its thread in the girl's hand. She whistled. The thread grew taut as the spool wound itself back through the hedge and leaped into her hand.

"Remarkable!" said Theseus.

"Daedalus gave it to me so I could find my way in and out of the maze. I want you to have it. Leave the Labyrinth tonight and try to make your way to the coast."

"You want me to leave?"

"I don't want you killed. I'll try to follow you."

"Keep your spool, pretty one. I came here to fight the Minotaur."

"Do you have any plans for survival?" said Ariadne.

"My only chance is to do what I do best."

"What's that?"

"Riding," said Theseus.

"They won't give you a horse. Just a weapon."

"Yes, but you can help me."

"How?"

"You'll be aboard a bull, you say."

"Yes."

"Listen carefully . . ."

She listened, then departed, leaving the spool with him.

10

Hero Meets Monster

The bullring at Knossos was a huge grass oval enclosed by stone steps shelving up tier by tier to the height of a hundred feet. The royal box was a pediment of rose marble on which stood a throne of onyx and gold. A white silken canopy supported by four ivory posts shaded the throne.

Here sat Minos, holding a golden scepter topped by an enormous ruby. He had chosen this stone, it was rumored, because he occasionally expressed displeasure by braining a courtier, and rubies do not show blood. In truth, save for his occasional fits, Minos rarely lost control. But neither did he discourage rumors that fed fear.

Stationed around the royal seat was the King's Guard. Each man wore breastplate and greaves and bore the double-ax, but had been given leave to omit the helmet. No man, however strong, could stand for so many hours under the Cretan sun with his head stewing in a brass pot.

Some hundred thousand people jammed the arena. The lower steps were reserved for nobility; the lower your station, the higher you had to climb. The crowd had been filing into the stadium since dawn. Squabbles flared up from time to time, and more than one early comer was hurled a hundred feet to the chariot road outside the arena. When this happened, the bullpen slaves would untether a pair of vultures kept for such occasions and the great birds would rummage the corpse, leaving only bones, which were flung to the mastiffs. All this was done with dispatch; the king disliked mess.

Nor was the purpose of the day forgotten by the multitude. People kept looking up at the sky. Surely, with such splendid appeasements under way, the angry god, whoever it was, would feel his wrath cooling and send a few clouds. But the sky was clear, so hot a blue it was almost white, and the sun was a wheel of fire.

Minos raised his scepter, then lowered it. The rites began.

A double file of oxen ambled into the arena—huge, clean beasts with luminous eyes and gilded horns. Perched on them were lithe youths and maidens, the bull dancers of Crete. Chosen for their beauty and grace, they were taken from their parents when very young and trained for years. The girls began performing at fourteen, the boys at seventeen; after that, it was thought, their skills declined.

A last pair of oxen walked the circuit; then beasts and dancers stood motionless as the priestesses took up their complaint. Drums began. The wailing turned into shrieks, mounting higher and higher. Suddenly, all sound ceased. A hush fell upon the vast crowd.

A white bull walked into the ring. Riding him was Ariadne, clad only in her long black hair. She rode slowly through the pulsing silence, looking very young and slender on that mountain of throbbing muscle. Suddenly the silence broke. The crowd was yelling, sobbing. Many people sobbing together make a sound rarely heard, an unbearable sound, which grew and grew as the people called to the sky for mercy. For the crowd was caught up in a delirium of belief. The mime of bull and maiden was more real to them than their own parched knowledge. It was life itself.

The maiden was Europa returned, which meant that the bull contained something of Zeus—enough, perhaps, to bring rain.

The maiden did not seem to be guiding the bull. Swaying there, slender as a wand, she was vibrantly passive. Every eye was on her; every heart thudded with her own. Each woman felt her spirit yield to the burning god. Every man yearned for Ariadne—thirsted for her, as for rain.

Unseen, the priestesses began to wail again.

Theseus entered the arena. A great hush fell upon the crowd. He walked in, unescorted, wearing a white tunic and a chaplet of roses picked by Ariadne. His single weapon was a hawthorn branch sharpened to a needle point. He walked slowly toward the white bull. Ariadne stood upright on the animal's back and stretched her arms to the sky.

The Minotaur appeared. People gasped in fear. Children shrieked. Light danced on the points of his horns. His sharp hooves glinted on the grass. When he clenched his hands, they were fists of bone. He walked slowly, stalking. He belonged to the sun; every hair of his fleece glittered like a red-hot filament. He was burning and terrible, a sun demon as deadly as drought.

Theseus reached the bull. Suddenly, Ariadne leaped off. She flashed away and vanished into the shadow at the base of the wall. And Theseus was standing on the bull. It was done so swiftly and with such certainty that the crowd thought it part of a new ritual.

For the first moment, Minos was nailed to his throne by

A pair of vultures kept for such occasions . . . would rummage the corpse.

amazement. Then such a gust of wrath took him that his senses fused and he fell into a foaming fit. He slumped off the throne and writhed on the pediment. But no one came to him, for this was a sacred occasion and everyone believed that their sacred king, like many a prophet, was responding to divine inspiration with gibbering frenzy.

Besides, everyone was far too occupied watching Theseus ride the bull. It is very difficult to ride a bull that does not want to be ridden, and this one was the largest and most powerful in all Crete.

It bucked. It reared. It stood on its forehooves and tilted itself up, almost somersaulting, then leaped into the air and came down on all four hooves in a spine-cracking jolt. But Theseus clung to its back. He had begun riding before he could walk. What he rode were the enormous colts sired by the surf stallions of Poseidon, and these colts had been as big as wild stags and much meaner.

Now, in the ring at Knossos, he was riding for his life against the Minotaur. He balanced himself on the bull's back like a gull on the deck of a pitching vessel, sliding down and bracing his feet against the horns when the bull stood on its forehooves. Theseus leaped when the bull leaped, landing on his back with his knees bent when he came down. He kept to the middle of its broad back, for the bull sometimes rushed at the walls trying to scrape him off, and wrenched its head about, trying to catch him with its horns. But he managed to balance himself lightly, never looking at the bull but guiding himself by its movements, for he didn't dare take his eyes off the Minotaur.

The monster simply waited. He crouched in the center of the ring and waited, pivoting slowly as the bull circled. The bull stopped, stood there with head lowered, rolling its red eyes. Uttering a howl, the Minotaur charged. Theseus stood on the bull. As the monster came close, he leaped off backward, landing behind the bull's stringy tail, which he seized and wrung with a cruel, expert twist.

The bull went mad and charged. Envenomed blood rose in the Minotaur like a gorge. He lowered his head and locked horns with the bull. The huge crowd churned with excitement as bull wrestled half bull—all except Minos, who was sprawled unconscious in the royal box.

Fettered head to head, bull and Minotaur strove with their horns. Theseus leaped back onto the bull and stood behind the hump of muscle. He jabbed his sharpened branch into the bull's flank, drawing blood, but not enough to weaken the animal. The bull flung its head up, lifting the Minotaur, and hurled him off with a shake of its horns. The Minotaur landed on his feet, darted back, leaped above the bull's head and with a vicious sideways kick drove a hoof into Theseus.

Things slowed for the lad. The Minotaur seemed to float up to him, moving his leg slowly and gracefully, as if underwater. But Theseus could not dodge this slowness. He felt the hoof slicing into his side. He knew he was badly hurt. The pain had not yet started, but he knew how it would be. He was slipping now in his own blood.

Clutching to consciousness with all his will, clutching the hawthorn stick with the waning strength of his hand, he slid off the bull.

The animal loomed above him. Its underside was strangely pathetic. Through its legs Theseus saw the Minotaur coming, slowly, stalking. He wondered dully whether the monster meant to kill him with horns, hooves, or fists—or simply by wringing his neck like a chicken. He knew his only chance was to goad the bull intolerably, making it attack again.

He struck upward with his stake, jabbing the bull in its most sensitive spot. In the split second that followed, he knew he had done the worst possible thing. The bull rose in the air with an agonized bellow and came down on him with all its weight. He felt his ribs go. He was crushed under the animal's bulk; he could hardly breathe. Every breath was fire; he knew that a splinter of rib must have pierced his lung.

Then he felt the weight lifting. He breathed deeply and almost fainted from the pain. The Minotaur was standing above him. It would be over quickly now.

But the monster was in no hurry. His golden eyes burned down at Theseus. Ariadne's half brother, this Horned Man. So strange. . . . He wondered at the strength of the monster who could lock horns with the bull. Where was the bull? It had trotted off and seemed to have lost interest. Theseus started to swoon. The Minotaur lifted his hoof.

"So he's choosing the most humiliating way," thought Theseus. "Trampling me to bloody rags on the grass. Why should it be worse to suffer a kick than a blow? Is death by hoof more shameful than death by hand? But death, that's what swallows everything—options, questions, regrets, and all the pain."

The hoof was poised above his throat. When the monster stamped, Theseus knew, the razor-sharp hoof would shear through his neck, slicing off his head like an executioner's ax. "Poseidon, help me," he whispered.

With the last flicker of his strength, he reached into his pouch and pulled out the spool Ariadne had given him. How slowly it came out of the bag; it was heavy as a chariot wheel. He dropped it at the feet of the Minotaur. It lay there. The Minotaur spurned it, then raised his hoof again above the crouching Theseus, who feebly tried to whistle the hedge lark melody that he had heard Ariadne whistle to the spool.

Suddenly, the spool leaped into motion. It rolled, unwinding its thread, circling the Minotaur, slowly rising and spinning a cocoon around the monster's body. The bull-man stood as if entranced while the almost invisible thread was binding his strength. He bellowed, thrashed, and tried to tear himself loose. But the thread cut like wire as it wrapped him close, tethering him to himself. In an amazing burst of power, the Minotaur flexed his bound legs and leaped, rising straight into the air and trying to come down on Theseus with his hooves.

He landed near the boy's face. Theseus realized that the Minotaur was still very dangerous, shackled though he was. He pulled himself to his feet, feeling his broken ribs stab him with every panting breath. He grasped his stick and thrust it between the Minotaur's legs, tumbling him to the ground. Then, as his foe lay there, struggling to arise, he lifted the sharpened stick.

A wave of nausea took him; he was swept by dizziness and he knew he was about to swoon. With a last effort, he tilted his stick, managing to aim its point at the Minotaur's throat. He fell, driving the stake into the monster's throat, pinning him to the earth and holding him there as the Minotaur's lifeblood drained away.

Theseus lay across the body of his foe.

It was then that Poseidon allowed his tides to release their pent vapors to the thirsty sky, which immediately darkened. Thunder growled, becoming sweet music to the people below. Everyone in the arena gaped in joyous wonder at the sky, which was turning now into one huge purple-black bruise edged with lightning.

Rain fell in clumps. The clumps became rods, lances of rain that merged into a solid wall of water. It was as if the entire sea had been lifted from its bed and hurled down on the island. The plains flooded; the valleys filled. Whole villages were submerged. People fled to the hills.

The bullring was a great stone bowl; the water was rising with deadly speed. People scrambled up the steps as the water pursued them. Those on the high steps fought to keep their places. And again the weaker ones were hurled off the top tiers; they fell into swirling water and drowned before they had finished thanking the gods for sending rain.

Thunder growled. . . . Rain fell in clumps. . . . People fled to the hills. The Barley-hag was squatting now in a tiny boat, cackling happily.

Ariadne had pulled Theseus onto the bull's back. The great beast swam easily out of the arena, across the flooded plain, and into the sea.

Theseus lay in a swoon, bleeding. Ariadne tied him to the bull's horns and began to stitch his wounds with Daedalus's thread. And tried to make the bull go faster; she had spotted her little sister swimming after them.

These three young people, swimming away from an evil kingdom toward their future, were observed by another who read that future clearly. It was the Barley-hag, who had escaped drowning by muttering a quick spell that changed her hut into a skiff. She was squatting now in the tiny boat, cackling happily.

"He will marry them both, one after the other. They will share his glory but die their own deaths. For today he elopes with the king's daughters; tomorrow, he'll sail back and help himself to the rest of Crete. Yes-s-s . . . young Theseus will return to Athens, inherit his father's kingdom, and assemble a mighty war fleet. He will defeat Minos in a great battle and snatch the crown off his head and put it on his own. Heh, heh, heh . . . I see what I see and I know what I know. And what I say is always so. . . ."

Now, as the wounded young prince and the two princesses sailed away toward that magic line where the sea meets the sky, the muttering of the prophetic hag became clear: Theseus was the kind of young hero who would risk everything and endure anything to make his dreams come true. Years before, observing the agony of his father's defeat by Minos, he had vowed that one day he would stand in the throne room of the palace at Knossos, dictating terms of surrender to Minos. And it would happen just that way.

Defeating the monstrous bull-man called the Minotaur was only the first test in his long quest for glory, and one that he almost failed.

Acknowledgments

Letter Cap Illustrations by Hrana L. Janto

Opposite page 1, SKELETON, *Roman mosaic*
  Courtesy of The National Museum, Naples
    Photo: Scala/Art Resource

Page 3, GIRLS UNDER TREES, *mural from Minos Palace, Crete, (ca. 1500 B.C.)*
  Courtesy of Michos Tzovaras/Art Resource

Page 5, OLD MARKET WOMAN, *marble statue from Rome (2nd century B.C.)*
  Courtesy of The Metropolitan Museum of Art, New York. Rogers Fund, 1909 (09.39)

Page 6, BOY AT THE SEA, *oil painting by Hippolyte Flandrin (1809–1864)*
  Courtesy of The Louvre, Paris
    Photo: Art Resource

Page 9, POSEIDON, *detail from ceiling fresco by Luca Giordano (1632–1705)*
  Courtesy of the Palazzo Medici Riccardi, Florence
    Photo: Scala/Art Resource

Page 12, WOMAN IN PROFILE, *drawing by Gustav Klimt (1862–1918)*
  Courtesy of The Museum of Modern Art, New York. The Joan and Lester Avnet Collection

Page 14, THE OLD KING, *oil painting by Georges Rouault* (1871–1958)
  Courtesy of The Carnegie Museum of Art, Pittsburgh. Patrons Art Fund

Page 16, THE RAPE OF EUROPA, *oil painting by Titian (1488/90–1576)*
  Courtesy of The Isabella Stewart Gardner Museum, Boston
    Photo: Heins/Art Resource

Page 18, MOTHER AND CHILD, *Hellenistic sculpture (ca. 323–100 B.C.)*
  Courtesy of The Museo Campano, Capua
    Photo: Scala/Art Resource

Page 21, GIOVE SERPATIDE, *Greco-Roman sculpture*
  Courtesy of The Vatican Museum
    Photo: Alinari/Art Resource

Page 22, BULL'S HEAD, *Minoan sculpture (ca. 1600–1450 B.C.)*
    Courtesy of The Heraclion Museum, Crete
        Photo: Scala/Art Resource

Page 24, APHRODITE, *statue from Pompeii*
    Courtesy of The National Museum, Naples
        Photo: Scala/Art Resource

Page 27, BOATS, *fresco from Akrotiri, Thera (ca. 2000–1450 B.C.)*
    Courtesy of The National Museum, Athens
        Photo: Art Resource

Page 28, VENUS WITH A MIRROR, *oil painting by Titian*
    Courtesy of the National Gallery of Art, Washington, D.C., Andrew W. Mellon
Collection
        Photo: Art Resource

Page 33, PASIPHAE, *ancient fresco*
    Courtesy of The Vatican, Museo Profano
        Photo: Alinari/Art Resource

Page 34, DAEDALUS AND PASIPHAE, *fresco from Pompeii (ca. 63–79 A.D.)*
    Courtesy of Scala/Art Resource

Page 36, THE MINOTAUR, *painting by George Frederick Watts (1817–1904)*
    Courtesy of The Tate Gallery, London
        Photo: Bridgeman Art Library/Art Resource

Page 39, PASIPHAE, *oil painting by Jackson Pollock (1912–1956)*
    Courtesy of The Metropolitan Museum of Art, New York. Purchase, 1982
(1982.20)

Page 40, MINOTAUROMACHY, *etching by Pablo Picasso (1935)*
    Courtesy of Collection, The Museum of Modern Art, New York. Purchase fund.

Page 42, MINOTAURE, *collage by Pablo Picasso (1933)*
    Courtesy of Collection, The Museum of Modern Art, New York. Gift of Mr. and
Mrs. Alexandre P. Rosenberg

Pages 44–45, THE TOREADOR FRESCO, *Minoan (ca. 1500 B.C.)*
    Courtesy of the Heraclion Museum, Crete
        Photo: Scala/Art Resource

Page 46, BURIAL, *oil painting by Bradley Walker Tomlin (1899–1953)*
    Courtesy of The Metropolitan Museum of Art. Georges A. Hearn Fund, 1943
(43.159.5)

Page 48, VIEW OF THE PORT OF A SEASIDE VILLA, *fresco from Pompeii*
    Courtesy of The National Museum, Naples
        Photo: Art Resource

Page 51, Detail from THESEUS VASE
    Courtesy of The Archaelogy Museum, Florence
        Photo: Scala/Art Resource

Page 52, CHARIOTEER, *bronze statue from the Sanctuary of Apollo at Delphi (ca. 470 B.C.)*
    Courtesy of The Archaelogy Museum, Delphi
        Photo: Nimatallah/Art Resource

Page 55, A CHAINED PRISONER, *etching by Francisco Goya (1746–1828)*
Courtesy of The Musée Bonnatt, Bayonne, France
Photo: Art Resource

Page 58, ARIADNE, *Greco-Roman sculpture*
Courtesy of The Museo Capitalino, Rome
Photo: Alinari/Art Resource

Page 62, HEAD OF A WOMAN, *Minoan sculpture*
Courtesy of The National Museum, Athens
Photo: Jan Lukas/Art Resource

Page 64, THE LITTLE MAGICIAN, *oil painting by Georges Rouault*
Courtesy of Art Resource

Page 67, THE KING PLAYING WITH THE QUEEN, *bronze statuette by Max Ernst (1944)*
Courtesy of Collection, The Museum of Modern Art, New York. Gift of Dominique and John de Menil

Page 68, MALAGA, *painting by Pablo Picasso (1896)*
Courtesy of The Picasso Museum, Barcelona (Donation Picasso, 1970)
Photo: Giraudon/Art Resource

Page 72, MINOTAUR, *contemporary bronze statue by Claude Lalanne*
Courtesy of Claude Lalanne
Photo: Sipa-Press/Art Resource

Page 75, VULTURES, *Egyptian terra cotta relief from Temple of Ramses III (ca. 1500–1001 B.C.)*
Courtesy of Borromeo/Art Resource

Page 76, BULL'S HEAD, *cave painting from Lascaux, France (ca. 15,000–10,000 B.C.)*
Courtesy of Art Resource

Page 79, THESEUS AND MINOTAUR, *Greek vase signed by Taliedes (ca. 550–530 B.C.)*
Courtesy of The Metropolitan Museum of Art, New York. Purchase, 1947, Joseph Pulitzer Bequest (47.11.5)

Page 80, SEASCAPE, *oil painting by Jackson Pollock*
Courtesy of Sipa-Press/Art Resource

BOOKS BY BERNARD EVSLIN

Merchants of Venus
Heroes, Gods and Monsters of the Greek Myths
Greeks Bearing Gifts: The Epics of Achilles and Ulysses
The Dolphin Rider
Gods, Demigods and Demons
The Green Hero
Heraclea
Signs & Wonders: Tales of the Old Testament
Hercules
Jason and the Argonauts